Instructions,
Abject & Fuming

Crab Orchard Series in Poetry
Editor's Selection

Instructions, Abject & Fuming

Poems by Julianna Baggott

Crab Orchard Review &
Southern Illinois University Press
Carbondale

Southern Illinois University Press
www.siupress.com

20 19 18 17   4 3 2 1

The Crab Orchard Series in Poetry is a joint publishing
   venture of Southern Illinois University Press and *Crab
   Orchard Review*. This series has been made possible by
   the generous support of the Office of the President
   of Southern Illinois University and the Office of the
   Vice Chancellor for Academic Affairs and Provost at
   Southern Illinois University Carbondale.

Editor of the Crab Orchard Series in Poetry: Jon Tribble

Cover illustration: *The Jay and the Peacocks* (detail), by
   Victoria Maxfield

Library of Congress Cataloging-in-Publication Data
Names: Baggott, Julianna, author.
Title: Instructions, abject & fuming / poems by
   Julianna Baggott.
Description: Carbondale : Crab Orchard Review &
   Southern Illinois University Press, 2017. | Series:
   Crab Orchard Series in Poetry
Identifiers: LCCN 2016031626 | ISBN 9780809335732
   (paperback) | ISBN 9780809335749 (e-book)
Subjects: | BISAC: POETRY / American / General.
Classification: LCC PS3552.A339 A6 2017 | DDC
   811/.54—dc23
LC record available at https://lccn.loc.gov/2016031626

Printed on recycled paper. ♻

This paper meets the requirements of ANSI/NISO
   Z39.48-1992 (Permanence of Paper) ∞

Contents

*

Your World Is Harder than Mine: Instructions for Children Heading Off to School

If your dream comes to life
and the houses
on our street lift themselves up
and walk off

on their leggy stilts and find different
roosts
        before you come home from school
I will meet you at
the spot in case of fire
under the dying pine—whose roots are not legs.

But promise me:
if the gunning madman
appears in the schoolyard and your teachers

shout the warning
Shark's in the tank! Shark's in
the tank!
pick up your dreamy head and run

on your stilty legs
to the herd's heart.
Only I will tell you how to survive:

let the other children take the first shots.
I will find you
under the pile of bodies—alive.

Instructions for Our Children, Living among Internet Enemies

When they poke you with the sharp stick of *Speak*,
don't speak.
Wear your silence like duct tape,
pressing your lips together.
Numb up. Walk stiffly. Look through.
Never at.
Don't hate them. Hate is a haughty houseguest.
Shave your head, if need be. But don't
nick your skin.
     Remember that when they beat
the bushes, the birds fly up into netting.
If you realize, in retrospect, that you helped
assemble the wolf,
          tooth by tooth,
try not to blame yourself when it eats you.
They told you it was heartless and fake-furred,
     for a glass-encased display.
No one is waiting for you with lamp lit.
     It's a trap just as each moment is a trap,
giving way to another trap.
     And the miracle worker
was drowned at her baptism.
        The snake oil salesman
choked on his own purpled tongue.
There's no such thing as privacy
only the blackmail of shame.
     Say it again, *Speak? No thank you.*
Here's my tongue.
Who knew it was for gutting?

Today—Bored, Puckered, Lonesome—I Would Like to Order a Russian Internet Bride: A Trisonetto

I've read that to train my new dog—low-down,
guttural, beaten—who pees as an act

of contrite submission (poor sprayed carpets
so stenched)—I should clip her leash to my belt.

The dog will shadow me all day and learn
all there is to know about love. Am I

the pissing dog metaphorically
or the owner (or carpet)? Would my sweet

Russian Internet Bride have a belt? (Please
studded belt.) Would my Russian Internet

Bride teach me how to ask for cigarettes
in Russian—*cigariettas*? Would my

Russian Internet Bride walk me to the
Wok N Roll or the 7-Eleven?

Or past the mission men so that I can
explain—all bark—how Jesus loves them more

because their hearts are apple-candied?
No. I've changed my mind. Today with traffic

shushing like a good river, a neighbor
delighting in a table saw, I don't

want to order a Russian Internet
Bride. I would like to be ordered. (I've learned:

it's better to be chosen than to choose.)
Call me Juliya. I will register

at Maison Russe in Lisle, Illinois,
established in 1972

for nesting dolls, filigree glass holders,
cobalt teapot from the Lomonosov

Porcelain Factory, and we will eat
fatty edges, stewy stews, and drink vodka

with our Red Square wedding cake. Please hurry!
I'm awaiting you breathlessly, sweet-kneed,

my corns freshly filed, my body shorn,
in *NEW ladies*, and I want to be made

new in the wedding procession—a train
of long black cars, ex-Soviet-style,

with tinted windows beading in the rain—
my starred and striped (hungry pinko)

heart—so flimsy and crab apple–pruned
delicate husk of something that once was

it will begin (pitter) to beat again
(pitter) all giddy and dither within.

The Sonetto of Accidental Inventions

Each poem starts as a hunt for something else
like a replacement for rubber in WWII—

the birth of Silly Putty, a.k.a. Dow Corning's
3179 Dilatant Compound—not *dilettante*—

though also known for its shear thickening
like dilettantes' skulls. Poems can pick up

an image—cartoonishly—and distort,
blot dirt, shore up a table leg, secure

tools in zero gravity? This poem contains
Elmer's Glue and boric acid. Its lines

imply cross-links between polymer chains—
removable with rubbing alcohol, cod liver oil

or my young mother, knelt before our thuggish
atomic gods, snipping the roots of a shag rug.

This Deathy World

Today my neighbor sways drunk
on my stoop
wearing yellow rubber gloves and cradling

a curved saw.
After finding your dead body,
everyone seems to be inching toward death.

My first thought is this: she's punctured her small
stomach and has come here to die. But no

she wants help sawing down fat limbs weighing
on wires. In the hard rain, bent to limbs,

we take turns, the saw jaggedly gnawing
wood, my hands stiffened to cramped claws.

And I'd press on for her (for you)
                              like this until
like lost boxers we hold each other up

until too tired for that, we fall hard
together weeping in the dark, bald yard.

Poem to Your Wound

This is a poem written to your wound
because the wound is innocent—
                          your jaw
the same since childhood—made solid from
milk and the fine bones
                          in canned salmon.
The jaw
from your mother's side—borrowed item.
The bullet didn't lodge there.
                          It burrowed
into the wall; your father hid the hole,
                          taped it
shut with a yellow Post-it note.

The blood—did you see it with one wide eye—
a warmth
like the blood you were born from?
Did you remember your children being born?
At your wake
          no one spoke
of guns
          but when a wine bottle shattered
we grabbed our chests
                    and an auntie
said that you were the kind of sweet baby
who lifted the bottle
                    and put it into
your mother's mouth
                and we all fell silent
because we all saw a mouth and a gun
and it will be like this:
                    gun and mouth

gun
and mouth
scalding our hearts, returning

                         —gun—

even when

              —mouth—
we think we're surely done.

A Double Sonetto for Pyloric Stenosis

First—I was yawed open—surgeon-made hinge
the stitches prinning inside of me still

little memories of the knife—then pinned
to the fetid bed by the baby's pearled

vertebrae—bony as a shark's jawbone.
Then there was a baby's bloody vomit

and I had to give the baby back whole.
His foot fixed to a splint for the IV,

his foot pinking brightly, bulging sweetly
around the shunt while morphine ticked into

his new blood. It was my job to starve him.
The barium—so elegant—was slipped

to him from a bottle. We held him down
watching the barium ink down his throat.

I milked worry from my breasts—soft damp breaths
of the breast pump while they taped down his eyes.

We couldn't think of death—tiny caskets.
Instead we inspected pyloric valves—

noose-tight cross sections in medical texts.
And then he emerged in a plastic crib—

his temples and eyelids raw from tape.
Now the dressing on his wound is peeling

at its edges—brittle as a moth's wing.
I see the dainty scar, run my fingers

along the exposed edge of the groove.
Suddenly I can only remember

shouldering the lead apron—the heft
of fear—of sorrow—is heavy enough.

Claustrophobia: The Closet's Perspective

You had vicious parents. They beat around
this house like the angry
tongues of bells—

bells shaken in fitful fists.
And so I
took you in. My fungal world swelled

woolen coat hems blessing
your head. My own
gloaming
—that blue light beneath the door—

you knew it well
amid the boxed gloom
this upright coffin
of memory. Years

later—pregnant—I hope
you recalled
not the womb
—but me—
how hard it is to contain
a human being who has no view
of trees, loping wires, the yard—

soon I became afraid
of your curled body,
darting eyes, the breathing in—
the thieving of my air.

Agoraphobia: The Great Outdoors' Perspective

Tender neglect
you were sent out for the
curative air
so your mother's nerves could

settle
like mud in the fens'
lulling hours.
The wing-scurried air.
The wheezy rud

of Mr. Castille's face,
his lurching gate.
You realized you were a stone and this

rippling out went on forever.
Hedgerows,
mailboxes, laundromats. Incessantly.

Now—years later—I see you
            through shutters
acting as if there aren't worlds
within worlds,

as if inside the house that sits inside
your snow globe
there isn't another

snow globe, being shaken by a woman
just like you
alone in her narrow bed.

Taxidermy: A Translucent Love Poem

V. 1
We are bound inside of the taxidermied falcon.
[enter poem here]
The wings shiver just before they beat.

V. 2
The taxidermist's tools:
Bone Cutter Forceps
Magnetic Brad Pin Pusher
Horn and Bone Saw
Flush Cut Trimmers
Pinking Machine
4-in-1 Rasp File
Leather Stretcher Pliers
Basic Field Kit
Breaker Tool
Automatic Awl
Awl Needles: Curved and Straight
Ear Openers
Leather Toggles
Gooseneck Hide Stretcher
Fleshing Blade
Fish-Skinning Shears

V. 3
"An exceptional bird eye at an affordable price. T1SP glass eyes are
a good choice for commercial taxidermy work with a nice rounded
profile and a flat back with no wire. For recommended sizes and
colors refer to our artificial Bird Eye Color and Size Chart."
T. E. Bunn Naturalist Norwich.
E. F. Spicer's shop lined with deer heads.
Rowland Ward Ltd. of Piccadilly (1848–1912)
Edward Hart Anthropomorphic taxidermy—fighting red squirrels.
Greek for arrangement of skin.

V. 4

We are twin taxidermied falcons.
I'm still on the wood block, ankles cuffed,
hunched,
one glass eye eyeing you.
My carcass is just wood and wool but
this is still my skull,
I stand on my true legs.
(There's talk of putting me in
a top hat at a tea party
or in the crowd at a boxing match
between two stuffed red squirrels.
Does it matter?
Only the carpet beetles can get us now.)
You're already in your glass box, wings arched
head cocked
above a dead muskrat.
Remember live muskrats—
their warm hearts pattering madly?
The give of their ribs—wee and springy?
We are bound to the taxidermist.
We know his grunts, cinching up
his taut belly—oh, the buzz of bone saw,
the click of ear openers and the automatic awl.
Who better understands
a gooseneck hide stretcher
and fleshing blades and fish-skinning shears
and bone cutter forceps than we do?
But he will never know what it is to be us.
(Oh, jealous stitching!)
He'll never know how the wings shiver
just before they beat.

Lice: A Mother-Daughter Love Poem

We pour vodka over the lice combs,
red plastic with metal tines and magnifier.

I give you permission
at twelve years old
to call the bugs "little fuckers." We hate

the lice the way we hate
the cruel girls
at school. We agree we'd like to call *them*

little fuckers. Our infested heads
soaked
in olive oil,
we sit in the sun,

take turns picking bugs
from our ripened scalps,
dragging out nits—
one fine hair at a time.

My heart cramps
in my chest because I know
one day
I'll pine for these vodka-soaked tines,

the fine-tooth comb of love,
our hair as shrouds
blessed with oil. I'll miss
each drowned louse.

A Fibrous Asbestos Sonetto

for the few remaining occupants of Wittenoom Gorge

See: succulent cross section
of infected lung—
you are the lodged particles.
Tour buses

stop at the gem shop
and the tourists squint
above surgical masks.

How does it feel to be blotted off maps?
Asbestos has always existed—
Egyptian burial cloths,
endless wicks,
Charlemagne's tablecloth cleaned
by fire,

vaudevillian stage curtains—my own
father, his narrow face flanked by ears—
See: slide 4.2—

as he draws asbestos through cigarette
filters while my mother hovers at the hot plate,
asbestos-wired.

I was the child wearing
flame-retardant pajamas.
We all swallow death
but you know its name.
We can only guess.

Today, I Turn to Stretch Armstrong for Comfort

You,
blond and lonesome,
in your black swim trunks
can stretch and stretch
your arms around me.
You are small
and vague—sexually—maybe
that's one of the reasons why I trust you.

But—mostly—you know what it's like
to be
underestimated—
the constant tests

of your limits—
what it's like when people
assume your constitution is made of

corn syrup. Stretch, do you know
why you have
only a green nemesis and a good
dog named Fetch
and no comely stretch-woman?
Did it ever dawn on you
that a stretch-woman
would be redundant?
Look at me—
Stretch—
look at my pleated stomach, my ever-

expanding and contracting milky breasts.
Should I even mention
my various roles—bravos

for angel, slut, mother, prude?
You can trust me too—Stretch—
because I know
that your ad copy was written by non-
elastic men
brittle as porcelain.

Squish him—scrunch him
stretch him out. He always
returns to his original shape.

We forgive them—they barely know
they're talking about
your well-worn soul. If you and I

could return
to our original shapes—
don't they know that
we would have by now and

they would never recognize us
arms linked
crossing rain-slick streets
in our rubber skins.

Sermon on the Mount Today at My Failing Kmart: A Broken Sonetto

Jesus, look again at us huddled and
shuffling
your gimp, lazy-eyed,
pierced, and homeless.
Today the disabled men have arrived
in a van.
Blessed are their trimmed heads?
Blessed are their brown pants,
this one with his bulged left cheek? Blessed be
this coughing child, strapped
to the cart? His mother torquing his arm?
Here, even the shelves are poor in spirit.
The dressing room is starved for our bodies.
Our tongues unfold for ugliness.
We are
hungry, Lord, and we feed at the surface
of fluorescent lights
for green towels, spangled belts, bowling balls.
If so blessed, then why does this dying store,
its dusty sprawl,
why does it smell of bleach and woe?
One of the disabled men has thrown up
and he's crying now. (Woe to me
walking quickly to the exit. Woe
to me: there's some beauty here
but I can't see it.)
You say blessed,
Lord, all of us—hated thieves who must have
our receipts stamped
before leaving.

After Having Sex on Palm Sunday, Some Clarity

Here, have faith, pulling the bulb string—shadows sway
on the basement wall, or later, night

falling down on us like darkness filling
shadows among hills, my husband and I

meet in the empty bedroom—remembering
our bodies' holy oils, oblations,

hills are not falling down on top of us;
his body falls on mine; my body falls

on his—now finally I remember
Jesus said if he quieted the crowd

the stones would shout out and how he mended
the servant's ear—the new ear unfurled

pink, fleshy, not a brooch, not an old wound—
no longer deaf, it rang again with sound.

My Enemy, Unloved, Has Only Struck One
of My Cheeks: An Interrupted Sonetto

Nearly soulless with one burning cheek, proud,
I rear it for all to see: red, shining,
taut skin, a hard apple; my tender jaw
refuses to chew. I show my burning
cheek to everyone—grocer, locksmith,
local executioner, FedEx guy,
Socialist, woman holding shears. No one
asks about my hidden cheek. Who could speak
of such a thing in light of this glorious
wound, tilted expertly toward the sun?

(I ask my husband to kiss me softly.
I ask my children to salute the bruise.
I call my mother and tell her how
I can eat only pudding.)

My hidden cheek is pale. Only I know
that it could be made of fattening cream
and tipped to the lips of a starving child
who could feed, feed till full as a bleached bride.

I Consider Doubting Thomas at Pet Kare in a Sonetto and a Half

There is only love at Pet Kare. These girls
hold empty hermit crab shells to their ears

like matching headphones. These boys caught crawfish
at a pond and want to keep them alive.

One clerk holds our bunny upside down, blows
on the fur between its legs then pushes

until something pink emerges. *A boy,*
she says. But her manager disagrees.

No. Look. It's a girl. We don't really care.
The boys have their crawfish, mini-lobsters

floating in pond water, souls suspended;
we have our bunny in a cardboard box.

My daughter says, *If our small bunny dies,*
let's hope it dies within the first ten days

so the warranty gives us a new one or
a store credit to buy a bunny leash.

But it may not die, Thomas. It may not
ever die. The boys know that the crawfish

could outgrow the glass jars, get transported
to the tub, and then expand forever.

See how we believe, Thomas. We believe.

Envy the Atheist in Sonetto

His typical blessings: the luxury
of disdain—reason—candid bemusement.

Envy the atheist his benign shrug
his Sunday mornings—his soul unsoiled—

his soulless soul—its airy high ceilings—
his soul imagines not imagining—

not even soul as bowl of warm porridge,
not even soul as carpet discount warehouse,

as petri dish, as lifetime warranty
or root, snow, plague, prune, atrophied muscle,

not even soul as plastic bag shining
with the bloat of water and the glint of

pet-store goldfish—the thrum of its fins—thin
and rounded, blur, spinning madly within.

I Am Not in the Wilderness but at Home, Weak and Thankless in Double Sonetto

The day resisting this poem; the day
is tubercular. In a stark X-ray

it would bloom white and cluster in lungs.
It can only offer the promise of

quarantine fumigation, a TB ward.
I scrape the convalescent wallpaper—

douse, pock—tunneling through generations.
Plaster dust rises, and I can't think of

anything to love. And how long since
my nephew skied into the sign pole? Two,

maybe three weeks? (Was he blessed by the pole?
Are we blessed?) It took four men to strap

him into the helicopter stretcher.
His parents drove hours, worry-sick, not sure

if he was dead. The coma lasted days,
but then he woke up and said, "Hi Lulu"

to his sister, and he wanted to know
what time it was. He ate two sandwiches,

grilled cheese, and he was brought back to us whole.
A resurrection. Now this collapsed day

emerges, afflicted by nothing, and I beg
myself to remember my own baby

in the emergency room—shallow breaths,
red-cheeked, grunting, his heart a-skitter.

I was just a kid myself—dazed under
humming lights, terrified. And I know that

I'm weakest amid nothing—glue, plaster—
the torpid hunger of quiet passing.

*

To My Lover, concerning the Yird-Swine

Lover,

Don't let the yird-swine in.
You can feed them at the door.
Hungry yird-swine.
You can polish their teeth and sharpen their claws,
but never, Lover, never
let them in.

(Here, I am milksop and blur-blind.
        I'm an ugly welt. I love too much
my own filth.)

Somewhere there are deer
        antler-rushing the hunters.
There are dogs who love chains.
I love the yird-swine, Lover,
just as you do.
        I listen to them tunnel through
the family plots,
        gossip chortling their throats.
They want to eat up from the past,
paw and claw in our bed.

They know that you cannot love me and my
stiff knot buns, worn hornish.
        You hate me
so well—
    so thoroughly—
only because you have practiced

(rigorous scales, taskmaster metronome)

hating yourself.

Today, Worn and Broke't, I Make Demands of My Lover

My legs sewn up into the bed
                    love-death, love-blanched
and the window ledge appears—welcome, welcome!

Then you appear, lover
                (nursemaid, murderer)
a bare chest that pants, as if your ribs
are a spoked pump.

      I wear my hair in two pointed buns,
like a great horned owl
           (or plastic owl barn-mounted
to fear off vermin).
                I love you
hatefully.
Lover, I whisper,
shut your mouth-hole.
            Play me a song on the buzznack.

Up you go and I will surely die like this,
      scrawny, abed,
an azzardly child,
a burdalone,
if not for you, so fat and butterine.

Give me the glee-dream
before the flesh tailor arrives,
before I give in
to the leachcraft
and learn to desire the tight suction
on skin,
the danzy-headed lightness
from a slow loss of blood.

For Furious Nursing Baby

Frothy and pink as a rabid pig you—
a mauler—
a lunatic stricken with

a madness induced by flesh—
squeeze my skin
until blotched, nicked. Your fingernails

are jagged
and mouth-slick. Pinprick scabs
jewel my breasts.
Your tongue,
your wisest muscle,
is the wet engine
of discontent.
It self-fastens by a purse-bead of spit

while your elegant hands
flail conducting
orchestral milk
and sometimes prime the pump.

Nipple in mouth,
nipple in hand,
you have your cake and eat it too.

Then when wrenched
loose you'll eat sorrow, loss—
one flexed hand twists
as you open your mouth
to eat your fist.

Burial Instructions—Abject & Fuming

Bury me beneath the garden wickets
bordered by the flower-maws, their fierce caws
to be fed. I am nearly dead, too leached
to be a feast for bedbugs, now skittering
to my larded lover's back. Bleach our blood-
splotched sheets, fumigate the sun-stripped room.
To be true, there is no velvet echo
among slick lungs and palpitatious heart
held steadfast only by muscled rigging.
Our love is locked in a wintry hive,
intricately iced, like a cake dolled
with glazed pecans, rippled as cleav'd brains,
lonesome as excised nipples reattached
postmastectomy. No casket. Stitch me
into gauze like a silken cocoon. Tell
the biddies to snip-snip their fine mole hairs,
cling damp-and-dear to my ignorant boar,
his beloved tusks still bright though brittle.

Concerning My Lover, the Ogerhunch

Your eyes still gummed by sleep are fit enough
                     to see that beast, naked
in a window, curtains full-sail,
airing
his arm-trenches in the morning,
                his turtled back and
oddly hairless gunstones
            flashing in sun.

Again, by midday, you see me wearing a dress greened
     by the grasses.

I lie to you. This fubbery feels good.
             I've made myself
a gazingstock—no?
              Doesn't everyone stare and poke
at me—the Ogerhunch's lover,
            and what a glory hole
must I have!

    Your punishment is to sit, and whilst I confess
everything—confess, confess,
            then confess some more.

To My Lover, concerning the Shaking of
the Bladder Rattle at the Maid's Baby

Lover,

Pretend I know nothing of babies. My womb
is a Dutch oven—
hot, bright, and hollow.

We should leave the maid's baby on its blanket
to roll blindly
near the hives.

Better that than how I fist-shake
the bladder rattle,
its taut shiny skin, the dried peas clattering within

like lonesome orphans—
                    like the tiny babies that will not cling
inside of me—or you.

Don't you see how furious I must look
                              to the baby?
My head swinging
like a mad flower
over its pulsing skull? See the baby's eyes—
merry-go-sorry-go-terrified.

We're better off giving babies
the stiff glance so they fear
love gone so sour
as caked talcum that takes on a foul feff.

To the Rumor-Monger amongst Us

Your prune-mouth widens, oh dark speculum
of hate. Gossip's first sweet
metallic taste.
With the telltale purring in your throat,
the lushes lean in, bloated craws, agape!
Oh, the wizened wheeze of joy! This pitters
your sickened, ret heart.
I sit mute, my disgust a fat bonnet, tied taut
at my gullet. You don't see the pearl'd
slick you leave behind?
Oh, welder of filthy dreams
and lurid guess. The hatmaker once whispered
your father was a madman.
Furnace-fat, furr'd like a needle-nosed bat—
a nutter, a loon.
(Let it be the truth.)
How can I forgive a foul-sieve mouth like yours,
but to kiss it shut?

Happy Little Death Threats

Death threats hold no sway here as I await
the Good Mister, tailored in wool, buttoned
into well-postured-place. Oh, how he'll touch
me, pull up my nightdress, fit my breasts
into a tight gown, partition and plait my hair
like my mother once did. Arrange my arms
like a hinged doll. So sorry, my dear,
this body longs for pine wood, even if
an unlucky soul—buried, undead—I wake
and, sighing in the dark box, must decide
whether or not to ring the cemetery bell
and be hoisted back up into the light.
Would-be killer, you're no killer at all.
Fold up your net; time will do your trawling.

To My Lover, Phrenology Hobbyist

Lover,

That skull knot is my belligerence.
That divot my love of curdling—
slow milk on the still.
Work your fingers westward.

                              Westward!

That rivulet is where I only think
of termite nests. And the temples,
yes. Rub, rub.

                    Not too tough.

The temples store the memory of Daddy—
before rabidity.

                         Mother?

(Stop knuttering to yourself

                    like a horse. Hush.)

You know

          that Mother has drilled
               into every bone
making my skull a honeycomb.

               And where are you, Lover?

The pit, there, at the neck nape
               is for you, where the finest
hairs wisp and fan.

               Lover of darkness and light.

Lover—fanged and toadish—all bark
and bite.

          Lover—distended belly, my barge—
          watching while I grow my goiter
          in noonday sun
while you fondle and hum my funeral dirge.

To My Lover, about His Bouffage Eating of Meats

Lover,

You are no longer to eat with me in my chamber
on beef nights.
Your thin face becomes too porked.
Your pleated cheeks grow
                    like gladiola bulbs,
flared red while your teeth
mince, mince.
I fear you'll swallow
your own tongue in your delirious haste.
Then what will happen to me,
                 my fiddle-faddle
fatal-fetal
deathwatch beetle?
Who will purr when I give a final gasp?

To My Lover, about His Derelict Neglect of the Gate-Lock

The speculum
          widens
my life.
Yours is a narrow tunnel.
All dark.
And I hate your aboriginal
neglect of the gate-lock.
          Why not invite
them all in?
          My buttons are lies.
You and I both know
that I hide nipples
          under my dresses.
How else do I arrive
but nipples-first?
          Those button nubs
softly folded into
my dough-skin.
          Summer now.
Derangement
of flies.
This is my life.
Derangement of time.
Dis-ease.
Illness.
Ill-nest.

To My Lover, concerning a Cure for Barn Swallow Mites

Lover,

Be not a seek-sorrow. Miss me not.
                           The world offers task
upon task—busy hands
                           so your fingers won't
turn to idleworms.

Reduce your mind to a thimble—
tiny tin bucket.
                      Finger crown.
It holds enough milk
                      for only one dying bird,
which is enough, after all.

God's gift is this: barn swallow mites.

Lift the wings, spread the feathers.

Use your teeth.

To My Lover, My 'Klept

Lover,

Now air where before there was a thing.
It is not moths that make the holes,
     Woolklept.
  At the end of every day, there's night.
And at the end of night, there's no more night.
And this is your doing, Dayklept,
Nightklept.
And one day you'll take my last wheeze,
      Breathklept.
And what will you do with it?
    More jars in the basement—
one swirling, moist?
     Will you unscrew the lid
and breathe it into your lungs
when I'm gone?
    'Klepting, 'klepting, all that's left?

To My Lover, His Hair Thick with Bear Grease

Oh, you of bastard folly,
I know where you're off to,
bear-greased as you are—
        the brothel of plump stewed prunes,
lush and awaiting.
You'll return (love me not, love me
not) Lenten-faced,
        but your nose tells the truth,
it's a bright red grog-blossom.
        Abed, lust-laced, the be-good eyes
feel upon me. In me.
I listen to the maid
bluing my aged petticoats
scrubbing blood from my skirts
on the battling bench.
There's no need to girdle
my girdle with knives. No thieves,
nor window-creeps want in.
Never did.
        My breasts will never weep milk,
but if one did, that chalkpaste would sift
through the Babcock
thin and blue.
My mother told me this was known at birth.
I was the pale crier, the pointed skull.
(Your mother loved you neither.)
And I think of you
—hair as pomped as a bishop's hat—
and I feel a flush up through my stomach.
Lover,
my heart sometimes skitters,
and my ribs wrap it tight as if made
of baling wire.

And when you sway before me,
I'll show you my goiter, a blackened mole;
I'll find every fester.
My death hithers, all for you.
Love me in spite.
Spite me, my love.
            And when you say,
Hush, hush, hush.
I'll retract like a wood louse, curling
at the touch—oh, my bear, my beast,
my favorite thief.
        The ash hopper says *tick, tick, tick*—
water through ash, leaching lye.

For My Lover, upon My Impending Death

Motorous heart, quit me not.
My body—as murmurous rumor mill—
you know what you know and spill
what you spill. Fuck me. Fuck me not.
Blood of little feathered pulse
quickening on my wrist. Split me open.
Split me not. My tongue desires
bitter pills. Poison me now.
Poison me not. Deathy sleep. Sleepy
death. It doesn't matter which
because the deathwatch beetles
tick. Tick for me. Tock me not.
I love you now. I'll love you not.
Forever was never, ever time spent well.

The Practice of Being a Lamb

I like this: eyes on the sides of my head.
I don't mind: thin knees that buckle and pop

when hooves sink into mud. (A word on hooves:
not unlike my grand fuzzy platform shoes.)

I adore oily wool, its stubborn warmth.
I don't want to be shorn pink, raw, nicked.

But the neck bell—I'd like to see it go—
too erratic in my veined, twisting ears.

When the shepherd calls: see me, here, fixed
in the dumb field. My tufted knees now lock.

Hear me resisting—mouth-wide, tongue-charged—
electric tongue, detonating—rigid

and purpled—my hooves hooking dirt and weeds.
Tell me: why all of this heated bleating?

Jesus Wants to Explain the Body to His Father

I look at you through my punctured hands—peepholes
like handmade cameras. You're far away.

If you glanced at me, would you know that I'm
looking at you through the holes in my hands?

If we had a closer relationship,
I would tell you how much I admire

the way you fashion miniscule infant
nostrils and a skull so rich it will give

an echoey thunk. Oh, and how the ribs
fan on tidy joists. And what you choose to

expose—the soft backs of our knees. And how
memory latches to smell—(my mother

is tapioca). I love how you gave
such warmth to warmth—how scars shine like plastic.

If we could really talk, I would tell you
what I miss the most today: The wanting

to touch a bruise and a broken tooth.
The perfect fit of fat tongue in ridged mouth.

How—looking closely—you can see a small
version of yourself in tear-blurred eyes.

How an arm alone dies then tingles back.
And how—oh this—in passion our hearts fill

our ears till we are drummed deaf. But now
through the holes in my hands I can see you

looking this way—all glowing robes and beard—
and I can tell that—no—from this distance

it looks like I've only covered my eyes
with my hands pretending to be blinded.

Jesus   Explain[s]   His Father

        through my punctured   peepholes
     handmade

                 I'm
looking at you

      closer
         how   I admire

the
        rich

expose
memory

         scars shine

  touch a bruise
The   fat tongue

         a small
version of yourself

     alone

drummed deaf. But now
I   see you

this way—all glowing   beard—
from this distance

pretend.

Mary Magdalene and the Lost Body

I know this fit
of losing. Staggering
through the tomb
      (I want your body back)

she begs
the gardener with the dirty hands:
If you've taken him away
tell me
where you have laid him.
I've begged
this same gardener,
rubbed his mud-caked hands
               between mine

to see if the dirt
is blood. I've fumed,
             shoved.
But wait.
Turn back.
Begin again
          with all that's left:
two angels, yes, dimwits
unpolished
and a lonesome shroud
            left to rot.
One minute Jesus was aghast
airless, laid in the tomb.
Then his first breath—
a shudder of lungs—
            drawing the gauzy
shroud into his mouth
kissing his wet tongue.

Of Poor Spirit

I am poor in spirit, weeping
festooned
in grief—
like the disciples before Jesus

reappears by the Sea of Tiberias.
I am the nets let down. I am

the nets sifting
water silt. I am
the shrouded body tipped overboard

unfurling, unfurled.

How many days before
being eaten to lace,
being bitten to sinewed fray—

between body
and soul unfurling, unfurled?
Up above, the disciples aren't waiting.

They are reworking callouses, salting
wounds.
I am poor in spirit, hopeless

as salt. Disciples
as fishermen again—
how quickly
they return to heaving nets.

In Rooms with Baby

I have never let
my spinnaker gust
white bloom on the water. I have never

squatted in the swale. I have
never been
to Duluth or the Sax-Zim Bog. I have

never spotted sedge wrens,
a flycatcher,
the golden-winged warbler,
the bobolink.

Nevermind Cairo. Nevermind
Nebraska.
I sit here for you
sun through window

blinking. My brain mitten-clipped
to this world.

The warblers sing
Seetze—seetze—see—see!

I only know that the baby's eyelids
go pink
just before the coughing begins.

Aquarium: Love Poem #1

for Dave

The jellyfish—
pink headdresses, all glow
and flounce—lurid
turbans—bodies made of

bright gown—
pulse above
our children's heads like
thoughts that puff and glide—up
away from us—

do I have to say it?—like childhood.

Childhood
makes me think of your father

hooding your head,
a blinding hood. A hood
and then a chiding.
You learned to see what

wasn't there.
Sometimes I wish I'd known you
in childhood
—inside that chiding hood—

you would teach me
how to know your father
by his knuckles
and I'd teach you to bite.

Like blind twins
we would heat the tight dark air
with our breath
like moles that burrow to breed.

Aquarium: Love Poem #2

for Dave

At the enormous tank
of roaming whales,
you're mournful about the belugas.

When they kick their fins
you see a man's legs trapped
in their muscled skin
and I have to ask

Are you the man trapped, kicking
inside the whale's white body?
You say

Maybe. Yes. Alone
without all of you.

I say *We're trapped*
in the same beluga. Those legs

you see are my legs and your legs—
there's room enough
for us both and the children too.

We're small enough to
live within a whale.
We gaze down
at the baby
front-pack as cocoon

on your chest. So little
his teeth—pale buds
glow beneath his gums
—small bones of a whale.

Today, There Is No Time, Only Squalling Squalor

This house
keeper of me—these offspring who
refuse to spring off—
I'm weighted down

with stubborn cells. I move from window
to window
dragging the children with me

oh the fatty tide!
while people elsewhere
are starving—bombed-deaf—burned alive.

I have *no room*
to complain. The children
have teeth. The dogs shine.
Easter will bear eggs.

We'll toss the stiff yolks and whites
bleary with coats of blue dye.
Our precancerous moles have been
      dug out,
our skins stitched with precision.
I tap glass
as my husband props ladder-
to-fence. With our bright teeth,
blue eggs,
doctor-nipped corrosions,
we could live forever.

Don't Take Up with the Married Man

Marriage has loose spores
that barb the lungs raw.
Blooms are ill
—sporadic—the pollen dust

thick as sawdust
burrows and packs the heart
like snow.
Don't take up with the married man.

His face is rubied
due to the choke hold
on his desire.
His cheeks will turn blue

as a Christmas ornament,
as balls you diddled in your youth.

If compelled still,
don't buy a bone saw to detach him
from his wife.
The motor's whine will deafen

and numb you. Once free,
he's no more than a
piñata
strung to your ceiling. Beat him

with a broom handle.
Then torn open—
spilt—
his dusty (snow) drifts

will block all your doors.

If You Do Not Eat Enough Omega-3 while Pregnant, the Baby Will Steal It from Your Brain

The girl in the auditorium sits behind me,
reports this is why she won't

have children.
But I'd like to talk about
my own dirty thieves—
their boned hinges,

webbing,
pulleys,
a system of varied
weights. The marble work
of skin. Enamel,

those teeth,
each a white machine
muscling up
like razor clams.
The dough of thighs—piping

trim of dainty veins. Elastic innards.
Rubbery joints.
Electric wiring.

I've been broken, entered, robbed blind.
And you—
girl—
are a criminal too.
You stole your brain
            from your mother. Picture
her sagging hull—all toil—
addled, leached,
her broad bleached skull.

I Prefer the Earlier You—Dear Reader

Unfinished. Your lisps
not yet wizened to
words—dry, erudite crinkling of your lips

before you learned to dodge taxes, jostle
into nylons,
the chuff-chuff over hips.

You—banker with fattened knuckles—or you
librarian
dithering through the stacks

as if overseeing your own
ward of loons.
Beneath the tether of jowls
               loose and slack,

I see your childhood faces,
the sharp glint
of belief. I want that reader
          —not you—

pallbearer, staggering under the weight
of dead love.
What if it's only the two

of us, forever,
our fate: pruned—agog
as lampposts
murmuring our dreaded hate.

On the Masochistic Need for Criticism

I'm the woman struck three times by lightning—
who's still drawn to
a darkening sky, who

                              desires
the metallic laundry tree
in the open stormy field,

an addict
to shuddering skies
and that moment when

the skin is a bulb, the soul tungsten-lit
with longing.
I am the woman again

struck,
my body smoking. Come close,
lean in.

Do you see the fused clasp
of my bra beneath wet shirt,
my lips pursing a word

          —*Please*—as in:
don't leave me alone.
Why do I find my hand pressed
to window

each time clouds
are purse-string drawn,
                   air rain-sweet,
angling so for yet another beating?

For the Blind Botanist's Wife

We let the backyard go to field,
saw mice
swimming through it
and so we cut it back.

The mice came inside
to die in the walls.
The scent pooled in our bedroom,
lingered so
                          midair, overhead, bled
throughout the house.

I imagined John Gough, able to point

past the picture hung
to hide your fist-print
the shocked wall
pocked, headboard-worn.

He would know the scent.
Here she is. Curled dead,
pregnant, womb-spun
a week and two days gone.

What was it like to be Mrs. John Gough—
to be a woman known
by scent, to be

known like furred bees,
knots of weedy stems, discerned
by the give of your skin,
its fevered burn?

Today, You Leave Me to Go to the Store, but I'm Sure You Won't Come Back

The hungry dogs
stare at my knees, but know
my knees are not my eyes.
How do they find

the wet moving bits
on my face? I see
you in my mind's eye
dithering in the

frozen foods, casement doors
aghast, letting
the glass cloud, not yet decided.

If you could hear me
I would tell you this story:
Once my favorite nun hid
half her face

with a piece of paper, lengthwise. She said:
Look closely.
She moved it to the other

side of her face.
She had two different
faces. Just slightly,
but slightly is all that we are.

SAT questions said this is to that
as this other is to that
other.

There are
quarter-fed motel beds
that will dream for you.
Is one dollar and twenty-five cents
in quarters enough

for a dream of you feeding our dogs?
If you don't come home, I will find
that motel and pay the bed.

Today—Hauling a Family on My Back—I Think of Fitzgerald's Exquisite Crack-Up: A Resistant Sonetto

Dear-hearted, briny Murderers of mine,
take Fitzgerald, maybe after a meeting

with Gingrich, hunched against the rain.
Does he think of Zelda locked away

at Sheppard Pratt? Does he wonder if she's
compelled to try light Swedish gymnastics,

bowling, or billiards? If she presses her
wrists together, talking only of God?

Does he want to remember how she burned
her clothes in the Ambassador Hotel's

bungalow tub or hung the curing goat—
a stiffened carcass—salt sweating a cast—

oils pooling, ropes grease-slick—
in the dank Parisian elevator?

Does he want to finally confess, lightly
that he *did* let the clock run out in the fight

between Hemingway and Callaghan—ah
how Callaghan took the old bull down—

the stumbling hooves, the bulked belly, the
dancing bear of it all! Does his mind ring

with *emotional bankruptcy*
mortgaged souls?

Oh, My Fat-Sweet Murderers,
imagine
Fitzgerald—hat on his lap, head pressed

to the train's glass. I can see him from here
where I sit—bloated with a fourth child—

fretting over money and incoming bills
—reduced and reduced

until I fit neatly in Fitzgerald's
breast pocket. (See me there: folded handkerchief.

See me there: cocktail napkin
jotted notes, rain-wet, smeared.) I know that

he has burrowed back to his father
(I have burrowed back to mine:
sweet briefcase.

Mine: glittering mind chained to toil).
And his father is walking home

between two stiff banks of snow—
early spring in Buffalo, fired from

Procter & Gamble, how a dead man can
walk and talk and move among furniture—

at once here, breathing, and gone.
If I weren't so swollen, I'd disappear.

Please listen,
Dearest Deaf Murderers, I don't want to

die of natural causes—writing is
an unnatural act. But why do you

kill us off—one by one—sending us
into Schwab's drugstore for a heart attack,

burning us alive atop the Highland Hospital?

I've spent too much time courting you
when I should have been fitting my heart

for a toughened rind,
sealing my skin in batts of asbestos.

Interviewers Ask How I Do It

This is how—
with the children who have gulls
in their throats,
with the bludgeoning sun, with

fluorescent-lit ills.
This is how—wilted.
This is how—exhaustion
sewn into skin,

into my hidden eyes—while people are
dying.
This is how—on my knees, instead

of rising,
instead of cocktails, chatting
hobbies—
ships in bottles and therapy.

Instead of
waiting for clots. This is how—
leaning on the shovel
so its handle

fits my sternum,
a hooked fish, breathing out
a word while rooted to red dirt—
why?

Because sometimes
the children are keening
in the throats of gulls—
sky as winged skeins.

As Men Relinquish Their Manliness

Fuck you and your foul attar of defeat—
the limp shrugging, the bearish wag of your

heavy heads. You hand over the title
but this regret is all show. There is no

new torment, only old torments shuffled
to new people. And the shiny penis?

Is it worth it? The lewd opalescence—
its unwieldy pep—dangling then urgent?

This one with its hasty surgical snip—
the matching set: cordage soul, shale heart, and balls.

You're now a breed of bearish lapdog—
here's some doghouse bedding, an old pillow

to hump, and time to relearn love
while I refuse the brutish forgetting.

America—Let Me Be Your Gravedigger:
A Disfigured Sonetto

One day, lugging laminate floor samples,
your heart will stutter, crimp then sigh.

                              Your soul,

engine-cut, will glide, spinning slow circles
like a motorboat on a man-made pond.

I will return your body to swaybacked
grasslands, weeping wheat

(Wouldn't you do the same for me—
despite your hobbled march, your ugly
rubber shoes and sour pate?)

and you will become

the poisonous wax-coated milkweed puff
except for nonbiodegradables:

bridgework, silver crowns, metal pins from your
new hip. I will bury you with your purse cinched

to your bosom—lifelike.

                              (Like me.)

A prairie dog
will burrow into its fine leather hide—

a stiffened womb—all that you can offer.
Womb as home
                    —womb as grave—
womb as worthy coffer.

When the Girl Becomes the Bear

There's no terror like the terror
of the sensory-deprivation tank
(because you supply your own terror).
It will not be the men who kill me.
It will be the women
                    who hate the men.
When they cannot kill the bear, they blame
the trees.
I am limb-sawed, uprooted.
A mute stump.
The bear still roams—his eyes shine,
his coat smooth as if freshly groomed.
(By whom?)
In the tank, I blink and blink
into dead air.
I think, *If only I could be the bear for them.*
Listen,
if you meet a bear
                    who whispers, *Kill me,*
you will know my voice.

Acknowledgments

Agni: "Burial Instructions—Abject & Fuming"; "Today, Worn and Broke't, I Make Demands of My Lover"; and "To My Lover, concerning the Yird-Swine"

American Poetry Review: "Agoraphobia: The Great Outdoors' Perspective"; "Claustrophobia: The Closet's Perspective"; "Poem to Your Wound"; and "This Deathy World"

Cincinnati Review: "For Furious Nursing Baby" and "If You Do Not Eat Enough Omega-3 while Pregnant, the Baby Will Steal It from Your Brain"

Connotation Press: "Happy Little Death Threats"

Esquire.com: "Today—Hauling a Family on My Back—I Think of Fitzgerald's Exquisite Crack-Up: A Resistant Sonetto," under the title "Chiarella"

Goodmenproject.com: "Lice: A Mother-Daughter Love Poem"; "Today, I Turn to Stretch Armstrong for Comfort"; and "To My Lover, concerning the Shaking of the Bladder Rattle at the Maid's Baby"

Green Mountains Review: "Aquarium: Love Poem #1"; "Don't Take Up with the Married Man"; "In Rooms with Baby"; "I Prefer the Earlier You—Dear Reader"; "Today, There Is No Time, Only Squalling Squalor"; "To My Lover, about His Derelict Neglect of the Gate-Lock"; "To My Lover, My 'Klept"; and "To My Lover, Phrenology Hobbyist"

Greensboro Review: "When the Girl Becomes the Bear"

Margie: "Jesus   Explain[s]   His Father" and "Jesus Wants to Explain the Body to His Father"

Ploughshares: "Your World Is Harder than Mine: Instructions for Children Heading Off to School"

Plume: "For My Lover, upon My Impending Death" and "Taxidermy: A Translucent Love Poem"

Southern Review: "After Having Sex on Palm Sunday, Some Clarity"; "Envy the Atheist in Sonetto"; "I Consider Doubting Thomas at Pet Kare in a Sonetto and a Half"; "My

Enemy, Unloved, Has Only Struck One of My Cheeks: An Interrupted Sonetto"; "Sermon on the Mount Today at My Failing Kmart: A Broken Sonetto"; and "The Sonetto of Accidental Inventions"

TriQuarterly: "I Am Not in the Wilderness but at Home, Weak and Thankless in Double Sonetto"; "The Practice of Being a Lamb"; and "Today—Bored, Puckered, Lonesome—I Would Like to Order a Russian Internet Bride: A Trisonetto"

"To My Lover, concerning the Yird-Swine" was reprinted in *Best American Poetry 2011*, and "For Furious Nursing Baby" was reprinted in *Best American Poetry 2012*.

The quoted material in the third stanza of "Taxidermy: A Translucent Love Poem" previously appeared as an advertisement on Van Dyke's Taxidermy Supply website but has since been removed. Also, the italicized stanza in "Today, I Turn to Stretch Armstrong for Comfort" was inspired by advertisements for the classic 1970s toy.